TAKING PICTURES AND RECORDING VIDEOS WITH A DRONE

D1566334

TOM SCOTT

TABLE OF CONTENTS

INTRODUCTION

Drones are the hottest topic in the tech world at the moment. People all over the world have fallen in love with this new technology and want to get their hands on it.

From kids to adults to business owners, everyone wants to own a drone. While drones are not that difficult to buy, one has to keep in mind that these aerial vehicles do not come cheap.

You will have to make a good deal of investment if you want to purchase a high quality drone. Therefore, it is important that you don't make a hasty decision when choosing a drone and that you take the time to find the right one.

Drone filmmaking and photography have become increasingly popular in recent years and have transformed the video production industry.

They provide a unique perspective on many areas. Aside from allowing enthusiasts to take pictures and movies from incredible viewpoints,

drones provide even more variety by allowing users to add distinctive visual components to help convey a message.

When taking photos, most experts state that taking photos over can provide them with optimal results.

Because of this, more and more individuals are looking for ways to take aerial photos.

Fortunately, there are different options in doing so from hiring helicopters or perhaps opting for drone photography services.

As of now, some individuals prefer drones when taking photos since it provides wonderful benefits that can make their task better. Below are some of the following.

One of the main benefits of opting for drone photography solutions is you can increase your safety when taking photos or videos.

Of course, when taking aerial photos or videos going high is much preferred by photographers since they have a better and wider perspective.

However, taking photos up in the sky can be dangerous. It gets even worse if you will be using a helicopter. Luckily, using drones in taking photos can be a safer option.

Another benefit of making use of drone photography solutions is individuals can have better maneuverability.

There are cases when vibration of the engine, safety equipment as well as noise can affect you in taking photos.

Apart from that, these items can also obstruct a wonderful view of a city or area.

Thankfully, using drones can provide you with the best maneuverability you need.

The next benefit of drone photography solutions is it is easy to set up. Surely, when taking photos most especially in the sky, you need to make use of different equipment.

But, some of these items are hard to set up. Plus, you need to spend substantial time in thinking and setting up.

By using drones, you do not need to waste your time since drone photography service providers make sure that their devices are ready to use. As a result, you can immediately take photos.

When opting for drones to take photos, individuals can also enjoy environment friendly features.

For one, you do not need to disturb the nature with the use of helicopters. In addition, drones can reduce or even prevent carbon emissions.

Finally, you can also get rid of noise pollution. With all these features, you can take photos without affecting the environment.

Finally, making use of drones can also help you reduce your expenses. Opting for drone photography services can be expensive.

However, hiring a helicopter is more expensive. With regard to expenses in salaries, individuals can also reduce this since they can take photos on their own as long as they have drones.

These are only some of the benefits individuals can attain when opting for drones for their aerial photography.

What is Drone Photography?

UAVs (uncrewed aircraft) or drones have had significant advances in technology, creating devices for every budget.

Other than having commercial, agricultural and military uses, most of us use our drones as a hobby or for fun. They allow us to photograph and video from an entirely new perspective.

There are drones where a GoPro camera can be attached. And there are others where they include a camera capable of taking pictures in 5472×3648 resolution.

When using these drones, you will benefit from practice and flight exercises before you begin. Even then, when you feel you are ready, you need to know the rules and regulations.

You will need to follow these legal issues before you start. You may even need to take a flight test to become registered.

Safety Measures

Pre-Flight Checklist for Drone Photography

If you want to get started with drone photography, make sure you check this pre-flight checklist.

The popularity of drones has exploded over the last few years, and for good reason.

The technology continues to improve as the size and cost of consumer drones keep shrinking.

Although drones have many uses, both commercial and recreational, the popularity of drone photography has become one of the main factors in the growth of the Unmanned Aerial Vehicle (UAV) market.

With this increased interest in drone photography comes an obvious increase in drone ownership.

This has had some negative consequences as there are no prerequisites for buying or flying a drone.

There are no mandatory tests or courses, no UAV pilot licences, and no laws in place to regulate who can buy or fly a drone.

This is great for the large majority of pilots who are responsible and considerate. Unfortunately, there are always a few who ruin it for everyone else.

You don't need to look hard to find stories of injuries or damage to property caused by poor decisions made by drone pilots.

How do you enjoy flying your drone without making the news?

The majority of UAV incidents are mainly due to their pilot's failure to prepare correctly and know their equipment.

There are a few things that absolutely every drone pilot must do when flying a drone for the first time.

1. Know the laws that regulate UAV use in your country.

2. Read the manual.

3. Put the drone in beginner mode and practice flying in a safe area.

RECOMMENDATIONS TO HELP YOU GET BETTER DRONE PHOTOS OR VIDEO

There are also a few things that you must do every time you fly, whether it's your first or thousandth flight.

These are not recommendations to help you get better drone photos or video, it's an essential checklist that will minimize the chance of an incident that could damage property or cause injury or worse.

At Home

Before you leave the house to head to your location, you need to do some planning and preparation.

I'm a big advocate of planning your photos, whether drone or regular photography.

This is less about composition and subject and more about safety. There are also some things you must do that simply can't be done on location.

Weather

Flying a drone in wind and rain is not only bad for your electronics, but it's plain dangerous. It may not feel windy on the ground, but 400 feet in the air it can be dramatically different.

I learned this lesson the hard way a few days after purchasing my first drone.

I flew it too far away, not considering that it would require much more battery than expected to fly back into the wind, and the battery died.

I got lucky that time, but it gave me a scare. Learn from my mistake. Check the weather forecast and don't fly in the wind or rain.

I use the native weather app on my Android phone, but the local weather service in your country should give you all the information you need about rain and wind forecasts.

Time

If you're planning on flying your drone around either end of the day, you need to know when the sun will rise and set. This isn't just for photographic purposes.

Flying a drone in low light is a lot more dangerous than you might think. Drones rely on guidance systems that are critical in preventing collisions and landing safely.

Even if you like using manual mode, flying in low light could be catastrophic.

I use and highly recommend the PhotoPills app for checking sunrise and sunset times.

It also gives you twilight times so you can figure out when there will still be enough light to fly.

Location

When planning your drone photos, you also need to consider whether flying in that location is safe and legal.

Every country has different laws regulating how far you must be from airports, etc.

They're not there to ruin your fun, but to keep aircraft safe. Don't be the like the guy who's drone caused a helicopter crash.

Here in Australia there is a great app called Can I Fly There? There is likely something similar in your country.

Plan Your Flight-Path

Take a look at a map and figure out the path your drone needs to take to get from its home point to where it will photograph from and back.

Often this won't be a straight line, so make sure you're able to keep the drone in sight the whole time from where you're standing.

Also check the distance to make sure the battery will have enough juice to get there and back with time to photograph or video, and still have some to spare.

For this I use a combination of Google Maps and the previously mentioned PhotoPills app.

They allow you to not only search for drone photography locations but figure out where to take off from and measure flight distances.

Update Your Drone

Most drone manufacturers are pretty good at releasing updates for their equipment regularly. It's a good idea to check for updates to your drone's firmware and device app before you leave the house.

They often include bug fixes that increase stability, add new safety features, and help you take awesome drone photos.

Format Memory Cards

This isn't a safety issue unless you're like me and have a tendency to throw your toys if you run out of space on your memory card mid-flight because you didn't format it at home first.

Charge Batteries

This is a no-brainer, but worth adding because we've all made the mistake of forgetting to charge our batteries before leaving the house.

It's especially important when it comes to drone batteries.

You're far more likely to delay bringing the drone back to its home point when you should if the battery is less than fully charged.

This means the chance of it not making it home is much higher.

On Location: Pre-Flight.

Visual Inspection

Take your drone out of it's bag and check it over. Make sure everything is tight and correctly attached. Check the propellers for damage or wear.

Even if your drone has never collided with anything, normal use can cause wear and tear that you may not know about unless you look. This includes the controller.

Check Gimbal

Remove the gimbal cover and clamp and check that it calibrates correctly.

Every drone will use a different camera system, but whichever you use, you want to make sure it's functioning correctly before it's in the air.

Use a microfibre cloth the clean the lens.

Calibrate Compass

After turning on the controller and drone, calibrate the compass. This needs to be done every time you fly as the compass is a critical element of the drone's navigation and safety features.

Magnetic fields can vary a lot from one location to the next, so don't assume that because you calibrated it yesterday it's okay today.

Check GPS

Give the drone some time to find its GPS location then check the satellite strength. Set the home point, including the Return To Home (RTH) settings.

Don't ever take off until the drone has a strong GPS signal.

Verify Communication

With the controller's antenna up, check that it's communicating correctly with the drone. Check the signal strength and don't take off until it's good.

If they're not communicating effectively at three feet, it won't be any better at 3,000 feet.

Flight Mode

Check which flight mode you're using. Some flight modes are better for flying, while some are better for taking photos and filming.

You may want to change flight mode while in the air, in which case make sure you know how to do it before you take off.

Re-Check Wind Speed

Don't assume that the weather forecast that you checked last night was right.

Look for signs of wind at higher altitude by looking at the movement of the clouds or trees.

Use your phone to check current wind speeds at your location. Remember, just because you can't feel any wind doesn't mean there isn't any.

Visual Inspection of Location

Look around and above and make sure there aren't any obstacles that you may not have seen.

Static objects such as power lines can easily be missed, but also check for objects in the area that may be moving like aircraft.

Even with obstacle avoidance, don't assume that your drone will detect and avoid them.

It's your job to know where they are.

On Location: Take-Off

Start Propellers

Many drones have a auto-launch function that will start the propellers and hover just above the ground.

This is fine, but I prefer to start the propellers myself and check they're working properly before it leaves the ground.

Listen to the propellers and if they're more noisy that usual, stop them spinning and check them again.

Hover

If you're satisfied that the propellers are functioning correctly, take off and let the drone hover for a few seconds.

Check that it's stable first, then use the controls to check that it's responding correctly.

If the drone is functioning as expected, it should be safe to fly.

Monitor Conditions

Never assume that because you went through this pre-flight checklist it will continue to be safe to fly. Conditions can change quickly and you need to be constantly aware in case they do.

Monitor the weather and light and be ready to land your drone if necessary. Keep on the lookout for hazards that might move into the area while you're flying.

You also need to monitor your equipment and battery level.

Bring it back sooner than you think is necessary and never ignore any warnings that your equipment might give you.

Have Fun

Drone photography is a lot of fun, but being unprepared can have disastrous consequences.

As drone pilots we have a responsibility to fly safely and know when conditions require us to stay grounded.

By following these guidelines, you can ensure that you come home with your drone in one piece and without making the news.

By getting to know your gear and keeping safety in the front of your mind, you'll be sure to have a lot of fun with your drone.

The Most Important Drone Safety Measures

Drones are not just for professional photographers and hobbyists. You can even use drones to carry items to hard to reach areas.

There are many dos and don'ts that you need to get familiar with.

You also have to research which areas are safe to fly your drone.

Obey the guidelines and rules set by the local authority.

BEST DRONE PHOTOGRAPHY APPS

Whatever new drone photography skill you want to learn, there's an app for it. There are a lot of drone apps, in fact, and it's hard to know which one to choose

Airmap

A must-have for every drone pilot. Whether you're a commercial or recreational drone photographer, AirMap will have the right features for you.

Some of the more advanced features include drone mapping, geo-fencing and flight logging.

Even if you're a beginner and have no use for them, the app's location-based flight restriction info is vital for everyone with a drone.

AirMap has information about UAV laws in over 20 countries. This is especially useful for drone photographers who like to travel.

AirMap can also be set to control DJI drones, allowing pilots to map out flight paths and control their drone from inside the app.

Hover

Drawing on the valuable data from AirMap, Hover is a simple app that tells you if it's safe to fly in your current location.

This is good knowledge to have if you want to make extensive flight plans.

It bases this on not only air traffic and your position in relation to airports, national parks, etc, but it also considers weather and wind at your current location.

Hover also includes flight-logging features that you can save and send to yourself.

This feature isn't unique to Hover, but it means you can avoid downloading yet another app to log your flights.

Both for ios and android phones, this is one of the best drone apps out there.

Google Maps

As an obsessive photo-planner, Google Maps is one of my best friends.

It's useful for many tasks, including finding drone photo locations and finding the best places to launch from.

It also measures distances, and of course, figuring out how to get there.

This is often the first place I go to. Especially when looking for interesting compositions that you would never be able to see from the ground.

The topographical map in Terrain Mode is a great help to see the contours of the landscape better.

PhotoPills

If I could only use one photography app, it would be PhotoPills. This little app has far too many features to cover here. But many of them are useful for drone photography.

The Planner and Sun pills are incredibly useful, allowing you to see the movement, direction, and angles of the sun at any particular time.

You can plan sunrise and sunset photos, which also helps to know how much light you have.

The Planner pill now includes Drone View, which allows you to plan compositions based on your flying altitude.

UAV Forecast

If you want a drone app that gives you more detail about the weather, UAV Forecast is it. This app will tell you everything a drone pilot could ever need to know about the weather.

You punch in the information about your drone and UAV Forecast will tell you if it's safe to fly or not.

The app will tell you about wind speed, direction, temperature, and chill. You'll want to know about cloud cover and visibility, and especially the chance of rain.

All this and more can be found in this app, plus it's free.

B4UFly

If you live in the United States, you'll want to make sure you're following Federal Aviation Administration (FAA) regulations.

B4UFly is the app the FAA has produced to make it super simple to know where in the US you can and can't fly your drone.

It includes a detailed listing of every airport in the country and a 5-mile radius around each one.

DJI Go

If you're a recreational drone pilot, there's a good chance you're going to be flying a drone manufactured by DJI.

There's no denying that DJI dominates the consumer drone market, so the DJI Go app is an obvious choice.

At its most basic, it will fly your DJI drone and control the camera. That's just the beginning, though.

It has many features that harness the power of DJI's amazing drones.

Intelligent flight modes, live HD view, flight data tracking and logging, and the ability to edit and share photos and videos right from the app.

There are alternative drone apps available, but you should at least give DJI apps a try.

Tesla Field Recorder

This drone app does something I haven't seen any other apps do. It tests for magnetic fields. You may be wondering why that would be useful.

The compass in your drone uses magnetic fields, and if there's magnetic activity at or near your location, you could have issues.

I've had issues with this before, especially when I was flying on the aptly-named Magnetic Island, off the coast of Australia.

This app came in very handy then.

You can not only detect magnetic fields, but also record them and share them with anyone else you think will find them useful.

Litchi

If you're not completely happy with the DJI Go app, or even if you are, you should take a look at Litchi.

It's a great alternative, and many consider it to be superior.

It offers some pretty impressive autonomous tracking features that are great for shooting video.

Litchi's flight modes include Panorama, Orbit me, Follow me,

Ground station and Waypoints, VR Mode (Virtual Reality) and Focus.

My favorite feature is the ability to plan out your flights in advance using the Mission Hub on my computer.

Once on location, it will follow the path that you've pre-programmed perfectly.

It's one of the more expensive drone camera apps at $23. So you'll want to use those features enough to justify the expense.

Kittyhawk

Sometimes you just want an app that does everything. Unfortunately, that app doesn't exist, but Kittyhawk comes pretty close.

This great drone camera app will help you with pre-flight checks, weather, no-fly zones, maps with air traffic info, flight logs, and post-flight analysis.

Kittyhawk keeps adding new features, which makes the app more and more useful, but the be features require a subscription.

It's worth downloading and trying for yourself.

BEST DRONES WITH CAMERA

Drones have many uses these days, and one of the most popular uses by far is aerial photography. Trying to choose the best drones with camera can be difficult.

When choosing a drone for aerial photography, the three main things you need to consider are cost, image quality, and portability.

There are cheap, portable drones available, but the image quality won't be as good as of more expensive drones with camera.

You need to decide what's more important for your drone photography.

Budget Camera Drones

Bolt Drone FPV Racing Drone Carbon Fiber

• 3 WAYS TO FLY From line of sight, to screen controller, to FPV

• HD camera that will sync with the screen and broadcast a live HD video

• Seamless transition from traditional viewing on the controller to FPV viewing using goggles

• Durable and lightweight Carbon Fiber Frame

• Ready to Fly Racing Drone Set includes: Goggles, Screen, Carbon Fiber Drone, Battery and accessories.

- First Person View (FPV) piloting and racing to everyone

Yes, this is a racing drone and one on our list that offers FPV (First Person View). As far as choices go, this is an excellent place to start for a beginner.

What you'll like is the Bolt's different approach to design.

As it's a racing drone, so it focuses on aerodynamics as much as possible. But don't think that it doesn't take great images or video. You'll find 720p HD that streams seamlessly.

14 minutes of flight time is all it warrants, which is pretty good for a drone that can travel 30 mph.

Thankfully it is made from durable materials that ensures protection and durability.

Ryze Tello Quadcopter Drone

• Shoot video and perform impressive tricks

• A 5-megapixel camera records JPEG photos and 720p MP4 video

• Tello flies up to 10m vertically and up to 100m away

• Operates up to 13 minutes per charge

• DJI flight tech – High-quality components ensure stable flights.

• VR headset compatibility – Fly with a breathtaking first-person view.FOV 82.6º

Not all drones with camera are supposed to be educational, but they are meant to be fun. If they weren't, I doubt we would place so much interest in them.

One of the biggest benefits of this system, apart from its price is that it does not need FAA registration. This is down to its size of just 6 x 6 x 1.3 inches and its weight of just under three ounces.

The Tello can be controlled three ways: through an app, remote control or through the Scratch programming interface.

The Scratch programming is open source from MIT but is a little more complicated than it should be for first time users.

The Tello is a fast and maneuverable drone with surprising speed for its size. 20 mph in the fast flight mode, and it could stop and turn in about 6 feet. The 8 mph is more manageable and easier to get used to.

DJI Spark

• Includes a remote controller and standard spark accessory Kit

• 2-Axis Stabilized Gimbal Camera 12MP Still Photos/ 1080P HD video/30 Video gesture and Tap Fly control.

- Flight autonomy with obstacle detection subject tracking

- Top speed of 31 mph in sport mode up to 16 minutes flying time

- Up to 1. 2-mile control range control

The cheapest of the DJI drones on this list, the Spark is also one of the oldest. It's been available since mid-2017, which is old in drone years.

The Spark made a splash when it was announced due to its size. For a drone that's about the size of a soda can, it has some pretty impressive features. This includes obstacle detection, GPS, stabilization, and hand-gesture controls.

For such a small size and price, there are limitations. It will only give you 12mp still photos and 1080p HD video.

The battery will also only last for around 15 minutes. This doesn't give you a lot of time to fly, take your aerial photos, and land safely.

Force1 Red Heron

• 1-Key Lift/Land operation – easy to take off and land with the push of a button

• 120° Wide-Angle 720p HD Camera

• 360-degree flip and altitude hold

• Two rechargeable 7.4V 1000mAh LI-PO Batteries.

The Red Heron is a basic drone that would be perfect for a beginner drone pilot on a budget. It's an RC quadcopter drone that is small and discreet. Well, as much as you can with the sound.

It has a 13mp camera and 720p HD camera. You'll be able to try your hand at aerial photography without breaking the bank.

Again, the battery is pretty limited, only giving you about 15 minutes of flying time.

DJI Mavic Air Quadcopter

- 1/2.3" 12 megapixel CMOS sensor

- 3-axis stabilized gimbal

- 85-degree FOV (24mm equiv)

- 21-minute flight time with a top speed of 68 km/h (42 mph) in sport mode

- 100 Mbps 4K camera and video up to 30 fps

- Forward and rear-facing APAS obstacle avoidance

If you want an affordable, portable drone with a better camera on board, the Mavic Air is for you. It includes many of the advanced features of DJI's more expensive drones with camera. The ability to shoot panoramic photos, for example.

It has a 12mp camera that records 4K video.

Mavic Air gives you the ability to create high-quality images and video.

The trade-off f0r having such a small, intelligent drone is that you'll only get about 20 minutes out of the battery.

Yuneec Typhoon Q500

• Personal Ground Station with built-in touchscreen, Integrated 3-axis precision gimbal camera

• 4K camera /30fps ultra high definition video, 1080p HD/120fps slow-motion video

• User-controlled video resolution, white balance, and light exposure

• 12-megapixel photos with No-Distortion Lens.

- Does not include Aluminum case, includes one battery

Also a 2017 model, the Q500 is a budget camera drone that gives a lot of bang for your buck.

You get an affordable drone capable of capturing 12mp aerial photos and 4K video. It also comes with a remote controller with a built-in touch screen.

This is a welcome change from most budget drones.

Most need you to connect another device with a drone app to act as your monitor.

Mid-Range Camera Drones

DJI Mavic Pro 2

• Equipped with a Hasselblad L1D-20c camera with a 20MP 1" CMOS Sensor

• Up to 31 minutes flight time at a 44 mph max speed

• 3-axis gimbal for steady shots, 8GB internal storage, SD card support up to 128 GB

• Enjoy live view in real-time during flight and record 4K videos at higher bitrates with advanced H.265 compression

• Functions include ActiveTrack 2.0, Omnidirectional Obstacle Sensing,

Hyperlapse, Low-Noise Design, Adjustable Aperture, HDR Photos

2018 has been a huge year in the world of drones, and the sequel to DJI's most popular drone was part of the reason.

Along with the Mavic 2 Pro, DJI also released the Mavic 2 Zoom. They're essentially the same drone, but with different cameras on board.

As far as value for money goes, the Mavic 2 is pretty hard to beat. You get a highly portable drone with some of the most advanced technology on the market.

And the ability to take professional-level aerial photos and video.

The Mavic Pro 2 comes with a Hasselblad 20mp camera, while the Mavic 2 Zoom includes a 12mp camera with a 24-48mm zoom.

Both models are capable of recording video in 4K.

DJI Phantom 4

• Camera with a 1-inch 20MP sensor the onboard camera has been redesigned to use a 1-inch Megapixel CMOS sensor

• Five-directions of obstacle sensing

• Video processing supports H.264 4K videos at 60fps or H.265 4K at 30fps, both with a 100Mbps bitrate

• Max Flight Time Approx. 30 minutes

Up until the Mavic 2 was released, the Phantom 4 was DJI's premium consumer drone.

Phantom 4 is still a fantastic option. It's right for those drone pilots who want to create high-quality aerial photos and video.

It can record video in 4K at 60 fps, which gives it an edge for filmmakers.

Like the Mavic 2, the DJI Phantom 4 is available in 2 models – basic and Pro. As you would expect, the Phantom 4 Pro has more premium features, with a 20mp camera and ISO range of 100 to 12800.

Professional Camera Drones

PowerVision   PowerEye
Quadcopter

• Micro Four Thirds (MFT) system compatibility allows a variety of lenses

• Object detection technology uses an array of integrated sensors

• Detects flight path obstacles and sound an alert within 30 feet

• Highly portable 600mm class aircraft

• Control range and real-time high definition video stream up to 3.1 miles (5 kilometers)

The Power Eye professional cinematography drone is available in two camera models.

First, The "Power Eye professional" is equipped with a 4K 16MP Micro Four Thirds sensor with a Panasonic Lumix f 14mm F2.5 ASPH lens.

The "Power Eye thermal" includes a state-of-the-art thermal/natural light camera with two integrated light sensors and two lenses.

This model captures a spectrum of light not visible to the unaided eye.

While this system is not exactly compact, it is professional. It carries dimensions of 513mm x 513mm x 310mm dimensions and weighs 3950g.

This class-A bug allows for interchangeable lenses, giving you all the versatility you could need.

It comes with a dual view set-up and allows first-person view (FPV), viewable in a picture-in-picture mode or split-screen with the PowerEye App. If this doesn't give you everything you need, nothing will.

DJI Matrice 600 Pro Hexacopter

• Created for professional filmmakers

• Compatible with different types of gimbals including DJI Ronin-MX

• Build-in Lightbridge 2 and A3 controller

• Extended flight time and wider transmission range.

- Precise control via the DJI GO and DJI Assistant 2

- Upgrade through A3 PRO and D-RTK GNSS

- DJI Software Development Kit compatibility

Don't be fooled, this is not the drone with a camera that you need.

This is unless you are needing a very professional system for DSLR cameras. It is capable of carrying a payload of up to 13.2lbs.

The best thing is, it is compatible with all DJI Zenmuse line of cameras and gimbals. On top of that, it comes with the A3 flight control system, upgradable to the pro version.

It comes with six rotors for extra redundancy and stability, and six extra batteries because, well, you'll need them. Expect a flight time of 35 minutes, but if you combine the Ronin-MX, then it reduces to 16 minutes.

What you'll like is the retractable landing gear. This means those pesky legs won't show up on any video footage.

DJI Inspire 2

• Efficient workflow

• Sense and avoid

• Spotlight Pro; Compatible with 5.2K Gimbal Cameras

• Intelligent flight modes

If you're planning to create a high-end video, the Inspire 2 is the drone you want. You can use it with one of two detachable cameras that also use interchangeable lenses.

The cameras allow you to capture RAW 5.2K video at 30 fps and 4K at 60 fps. You can capture still images at 20mp. It also has an integrated SSD onboard. This means you can record high-quality video directly without any lag.

Inspire 2 uses a dual-camera system. This allows for two connected controllers.

One to pilot the drone and one to control the movement of the video camera.

It also features super-advanced vision systems to prevent collisions. This allows the drone to be flown indoors.

This drone is for professionals who need to create professional-level aerial photos and video. And have the budget for it.

It's not a cheap drone by any means, but if you can afford it, you get a lot of drone for your money.

Yuneec Typhoon H Plus

• 4K camera for video and 20MP Photos

• 360-Degree Image and Video Capture. 3-Axis Sensor-Driven Image Stabilization.

- Up to 1 Mile 2.4/5.8 GHz Wi-Fi Range. Flight Controller with 7" Touch Screen

- Up to 30 Minutes of Flight Time

- Intel RealSense Collision Avoidance. Intelligent Autonomous Flight Modes

- Can Withstand Winds up to 35 mph. 5-Rotor Fail Safe Mode

Yuneec upgraded the Typhoon H Plus in 2018 to cater to aerial photographers. The 2018 drone comes with a brand new E90 camera.

The camera features a 3-axis gimbal, 20mp camera for still photography. And the ability to record 4K aerial video at 60 fps.

If that sounds familiar, it's because those are the same specs as the DJI Phantom Pro 4.

You may not be familiar with the brand. But Yuneec's drones are packed with features and hardware that suit aerial photographers.

The Typhoon H Plus comes with an Android-powered screen built into the controller. And advanced obstacle avoidance designed by Intel.

ND Filters for Drone Photography

Long exposures from drones at night-time are very easy. A quick press of a button will allow the machine to capture a sharp image using its stabilisation mechanisms.

During the day, you will face a problem. Even by lowering your ISO and increasing your shutter speed, your image will be overexposed.

This is where the ND (Neutral Density) filter comes in. It blocks the amount of light hitting the sensor, allowing you to photograph for a longer time.

This helps to create a motion blur due to the longer shutter speed

How To Use an ND Filter for Drone Photography

A ND filter (neutral density filter) can create beautiful motion blur in your drone photos and videos.

It's worthing learning about the technical side of neutral density filters. With this knowledge, you'll be able to capture professional and creative drone photos.

The Difference Between ND Filters and Polarising Filters

There's a significant difference between neutral density filters and polarising filters. They're not interchangeable, but you can use them together.

Both can improve the quality of your drone photos. They have unique features that exist for specific drone photo and videographers.

- ND filters can help you achieve more motion blur in drone videos. They can

neutralise everything in your drone photos. They're not made to enhance colours or make skies look more dramatic. Generally, they help videographers create smoother movements in their videos.

- Polarising filters darken skies, reduces glare, and make colours look more vibrant. They're perfect for both drone photographers and videographers.

ND filters usually come in packs. Each ND filter has a different intensity.

You can have more control over the lighting in your drone photos because of this.

You can stack ND filters and polarising filters. Stacking will make your drone a little heavier, though.

A better solution is to buy ND-PL filters. This lightweight filter will give you every polarising and neutral destiny filter quality.

Invest in a Good Pack of ND Filters

Basic ND filters usually come in packs of four. They tend to cost less than $100.

The packs include a variety of neutral density filters.

While they all do the same job, they have different intensity levels.

The one you pick for your photoshoot will determine how bright or dark your drone photos look.

The ND filters are usually ND4, ND8, ND16, and ND32. The higher the number, the less light the filter lets in.

This means that ND32 filters let in the least amount of light. They are for use in very bright locations.

Make sure that the filters you buy aren't too cheap. Some companies seem to sell affordable and high-quality neutral density filters. These might ruin the quality of your drone photos.

Based on many drone photographers' reviews, a few of the best websites for buying drone ND filters are Freewell, DJI, and Fstop Labs.

Choose the Right Weather Conditions for the Best Aerial Photos

ND filters can also help you take great aerial photos in intense weather conditions.

The best light for using ND filters is very bright sunlight. If it's very sunny outside, you might need an ND64 filter.

Make sure you always have your pack of ND filters with you.

Depending on where you live and what time of year it is, the weather will likely change during your photoshoot.

You might have to shoot using at least two different ND filters. This consistency will keep your photos looking professional and fresh.

If you're shooting nighttime aerial photos, you won't need an ND filter at all.

Use Manual Mode to Control Every Setting in Your Drone

Manual mode is important in every kind of photography. If you shoot in automatic, the drone might choose camera settings that won't make the most of your ND filter.

You'll see a difference as soon as you put the ND filter on your drone lens. You can experiment with different shutter speed and ISO settings to find the best light.

While there are a few shortcuts you can use, try to figure everything out on your own first.

Manual mode is a great way to introduce yourself to basic camera settings.

Everything you learn will come in handy in DSLR photography. Consider this a general photography exercise.

Use ND Filters to Create Beautiful Motion Blur in Your Drone Videos

Drone videographers use ND filters to create smooth movements in their videos. Without motion blur, videos look sharp and fixed.

This is generally very unappealing to the eye. With motion blur, videos tend to look more professional.

Aim to use slow shutter speed. In bright conditions, slow shutter speed can make your footage look overexposed.

You have to compensate for that by changing another camera setting. For example, you can lower your ISO.

But what if all your camera settings look decent? This situation is when ND filters come in. With an ND filter, you can compensate for slow shutter speed.

You can get rid of overexposure and capture very smooth movements at the same time.

Best Memory Cards for All Photography Budgets – CF | SD | MicroSD

Your photographs are only as good as your memory card. It takes a lot of time, effort and energy to get your drone in the air.

The last thing you want is to miss that crucial panoramic shot halfway through a series due to a bad buffer rate. Therefore, you need a card that will allow you to have a fast writing speed. It is also better if the card is micro SD, as it is the size that is compatible with most drones.

Your memory card is in charge of rendering and storing your images, so choose wisely.

Drawbacks to Drones

Most consumer drones limit you to one focal length and lack the ability to zoom or change lenses. While "professional" level drones may offer these capabilities, the price tag of such aircraft are often out of the range for most photographers.

Second, drones have limited flight ranges, elevation capabilities, and are, at times, limited by regulations.

Some locations, like National Parks in the United States (and many other countries) are off-limits to drones. Limits to the range of drones means you still have to get close to your subject (relatively speaking) in order to get the image you need.

Lastly, countries across the world are creating laws limiting the use of drones. In some countries, it's almost impossible to get permission to fly legally.

In the United States, if you want to use your drone for any commercial purpose, including selling images created with your drone, you need to be a licensed unmanned aerial vehicle pilot.

Advantages of Drones

Even with those drawbacks, drones still have a lot things going for them. First and foremost is freedom and flexibility.

See some pretty evening light out your window and feel like making some aerial photos? No problem, just grab the drone and go.

Cost is another.

A charter aircraft can cost hundreds of dollars an hour. Two hours of flying time in a charter

helicopter will just about pay for a decent quadcopter drone.

You also get the freedom to adjust composition at a whim. Feel like making a shot from five feet off the ground and then your next from 100? You can make the change in seconds.

You also have the time to get things right. In a fast-moving airplane, the compositions can come and go in seconds.

With a drone, you can simply adjust the position of the drone or angle of the camera for as long as you wish until you get it right.

As long as your battery holds out anyway.

CAMERA SETTINGS

I like to think of entry-level to mid-range drones as flying camera phones: they can make lovely images, but are limited in flexibility.

Most drones have the ability to adjust colour temperature and exposure using an exposure compensation-like setting.

But they offer little manual control otherwise. Shutter speed and aperture are left mostly up to the camera.

One thing most decent drones do offer, is the ability to shoot in RAW. If your drone offers that setting, I strongly recommend you use it.

The quality coming from the small sensors of most consumer drones is marginal and RAW will allow you to make the most of each photo. It can be processed just as you would any RAW image from your SLR or mirrorless camera.

Drone Photography Composition

I like to fly my drone fairly low. I find the combination of altitude and wide-angle lenses make everything look less dramatic and smaller if I'm flying too high.

Twenty to thirty metres off the ground is probably my favourite height, but of course, it varies on where I'm flying and the image I'm creating.

Remember to take advantage of the many camera angles drone photography allows.

Shooting straight down is almost impossible from a plane. From a drone though? It is as easy as angling your camera.

Playing with lines and patterns is a drone speciality. Take advantage of the way the world looks from above and play with dividing your images into parts using the natural variations in the landscape.

Trees from above, for example, create a starburst pattern, not a typical way humans see a forest!

The flexibility provided by drone photography is extraordinary. Don't be afraid to experiment with aerial images of places a plane could never fly.

Warnings About Drones

Always follow the rules! Flying a drone around airports, emergency situations, wildfires, or areas with other aircraft is not only irresponsible but also dangerous and even life-threatening.

Be aware of the laws where you are flying and follow them. Punishments for violations can be harsh.

Last, be respectful of others. Don't fly over private property if you don't have permission from the land-owner and be aware of how your flight is impacting the experience of others. Simply, don't be a jerk.

Flying Exercises for Successful Drone Photography

A pilot has to complete hundreds of hours in a flight simulator before getting behind an actual wheel. Flying exercises are to be used to build up the pilot's confidence.

This is why they are also needed for drone photography.

They allow you to see what it feels like to fly the drone at a low altitude. This will help you avoid a bad landing damaging your device.

Knowing how to use your drone effectively will minimise the number of accidents and flyaways. It also ensures stunning images from your drone photography.

Don't forget the golden rule: IF YOU CRASH, THROTTLE OFF IMMEDIATELY!

To that, we'd like to add a second rule: fast flying is fun, but slow, controlled flying is how you improve.

These exercises are all about control and smoothness.

Don't try to go fast, try to be perfect, just like me. That's a joke. I am profoundly crap, as you will discover when watching the videos below.

Hover 'round the clock

Sack up, soldier. It's time to start working on orientation. The first thing we're going to do is try to maintain a stable hover while pointing in a bunch of different directions.

First up, practice holding a steady tail-in hover over a marked spot before messing with orientation, compensating for any breeze or any movement of the aircraft to keep it in place.

When you're ready, use the left stick yaw control to turn 90 degrees right to the 3 o'clock position and hold it there. Tough, right? You need to conceptualize the situation from the drone's point of view, always remembering which way it's facing and developing an instinct for correcting in the right direction when it moves off its spot.

When you get the hang of that, rotate back to the left until you're at the 9 o'clock position and do the same thing.

Everything will be reversed, but if you keep that mental model of the quad in your mind and conceptualize everything from its point of view, you should be able to get a handle on it.

Finally, rotate the drone until it's facing you and hold it still in the air.

Keep that mental model in mind – use the lights as a cue to remember which way the drone is facing.

If you're anything like me, this one will give you the absolute willies.

Even if you're fairly confident with the drone in motion, holding it still without stabilization and gently correcting for random breeze in a bunch of different orientations is a tough thing to get your head around, and a good reminder of how in control you really are. Good luck!

FLYING IN CIRCLES (BANK TURNS)

Time to take things up another notch and start using all the controls at once. The challenge here is to fly in smooth circles around a marker, while rotating the drone so it's always facing forward.

Position yourself to one side of your marker, give yourself a little forward momentum, and then gently add a little yaw with the left stick.

You'll also have to use a touch of right stick roll to bring it around, all the while managing your throttle to keep the drone level.

The key skill here is managing your momentum - a turning drone is like a car drifting on ice with zero traction, floating sideways until it's given a push in a new direction.

Use your right stick roll to nudge it around into a bank turn.

You should be able to find a point where you can leave your controls pretty steady and have the aircraft come around smoothly without too much correction, as long as you're not flying in the wind.

Got it? Great, then do it in the other direction. You want to reach a point where you can take off and go straight into a smooth circle.

For bonus points, you might want to try circling with the drone's nose pointing straight towards the centre of the at all times – a nose-in circle. I actually find this one a bit easier, probably due to years of FPV gaming in which the ol' strafe-n-circle move has slain me many a foul beast. Only, with gaming, movement is on the left hand and you change orientation with the right, so your gaming instincts will tend to make you go the wrong way.

Figure 8s

Is our numbering scheme appropriate, or what? For this one you'll need two markers, about 10 meters apart.

Building on your circle work above, your challenge is to fly figure 8s in both directions, keeping the drone facing forward as it flies.

Adding the markers makes this a ton more difficult than the previous exercise – free movement is much easier than putting your drone exactly where you want it.

Keep it slow, keep it under control. You've got more to gain from precision than from speed here.

Be aware of any cross-breeze, which will tend to make your turns tighter than a duck's bum at one end and completely out of control at the other.

Start out very slowly, just using yaw and a little pitch to get you around -

and when you start to get that under control, add in some bank to your turns as above. The more speed you develop, the more likely you'll spin out of control, so give yourself some space!

Nose-in landing

Fly out to about 10 meters in front of yourself, at a height of a couple of meters. Then turn the drone around and bring it back towards yourself, and land it on a pre-determined spot a couple of meters in front of you.

Landing nose-in means you have to manage direction, orientation and the ground-effect cushion while making a controlled descent to a specific spot.

There's a fair bit going on, so take it slow and go for precision.

Try an R/C Flight Simulator

Surely by this point you're getting a picture of how easy and expensive quads can be to crash – and how nifty you need to be with the sticks to fly one well. Luckily, there's an option for you that lets you experiment with all kinds of tricks – and it doesn't take two bloody hours to charge the battery.

Flight simulators featuring quadcopters have popped up all over the place in the last couple of years, and some of them are pretty damn good as well as being cheap.

We're not going to try to list them all here, you can do a bit of googling to see which sim you like, but I can recommend one I've been using a fair bit lately: FPV Freerider.

It costs five bucks on a PC or Mac, less on mobile devices, and it hooks up via USB or Bluetooth to a range of R/C controllers as well as gamepads like the Playstation controller.

There's only one flight model, but you do get a range of different environments to fly in, either line of sight or FPV (first person view) if you want to train up to do some drone racing.

You can fly in self-levelling attitude mode, high-rate attitude mode or acro/manual mode, and I've found it very helpful. You can adjust the physics to try to make it feel as much as possible like whatever you're used to flying.

SHOOTING DRONE PHOTOGRAPHY

Best Tips for Starting a Drone Photography Business

Drone photography is increasingly popular due to the unique point of view it offers.

So it would make sense for you to decide that you want to get into the drone photography business.

To make sure everything runs smoothly, there are a couple of things you need to pay attention to. These include researching the laws, finding the best drone, and having a pre-photoshoot checklist prepared.

Read Drone Laws to Avoid Shooting Illegally.

There are many drone laws to keep in mind when you take photos anywhere. These laws, however, depend on the country you're in.

For example, here are a few laws for American citizens:

• your drone must weight less than 55 pounds;

• you can't fly above 400 feet; and

• you must always be able to see your drone.

Being aware of basic drone laws will help you have safe and successful photoshoots anywhere.

This will also strengthen your reputation and make clients trust you more.

Start with an Affordable Drone to Practise Drone Photography

You might be tempted to invest in an expensive drone right away. Even if you have the money, consider buying a cheaper drone first.

This will give you a chance to experiment without worrying about damaging your equipment. You'll be able to focus on composition, angles, and views instead.

Some of the most affordable drones out there are:

• Ryze Tello

- Potensic D85

- Hasakee K5 Mini Nano Drone

Most of these are lightweight and have high-quality cameras, so you don't need to worry about compromising the quality of your work.

Later on Invest in a High-Quality Drone to Take Amazing Shots

When you feel that you have enough experience as a drone photographer, you can invest in professional drones. The kind of drone you choose depends on the kind of work you plan to do. (More on this later.)

These are all fairly pricey, but they're all worthy investments if you want to start a sustainable drone photography business.

The better your equipment, the more confident you'll feel when offering your services to clients.

Experiment with Different Drone Genres to Find Your Favourite(s)

This is one of the most important steps of your business plan. As mentioned before, drone photography comes with a lot of sub-genres.

Here are just a few categories that drone photographers can get into:

• Real estate

• Surveillance

• Agriculture

• Weddings

Make sure that you experiment with as many genres as possible. Have at least two favourite photography genres that you can work on in the long run. The more skills you develop, the more clients you'll have.

Once you pick a few favourites, you can start offering your services to a wide variety of people.

Create a Checklist to Ensure a Smooth Operation

Before you make your business official, you can make a list of everything you'd like to focus on. This can be a to-do list or simply a list of questions.

A few questions you can keep in mind are:

• What is my target audience?

• How much can I realistically earn in one year?

• Do I have any acquaintances or friends who might be interested in my business?

• Do I also want to offer drone videography?

• What is the best social media platform to advertise my work?

• What is my backup plan if something goes wrong?

The more prepared you are, the easier you'll find it to keep your business strong, no matter what you experience.

Improve Your Drone Photography Business by Looking at Competitors

Different kinds of drone photography thrive in different areas.

Look at local drone photographers and see what they're offering. Take note of similarities, pricing packages, and editing styles.

Do most of them offer photography services only?

If so, maybe you can offer extra videography services.

Your goal is to find what's missing and use it to attract customers.

There are other things you can include in your offer, such as professional colour correction and a 24-hour turnaround.

Of course, you need to make sure that what you're offering is realistic for your lifestyle. While it's important to take your work to the next level, don't forget about your limits and abilities.

For example, if you have a part-time job, you can offer a 48-hour turnaround instead of a 24-hour turnaround.

This might give you enough time to work on both jobs efficiently without compromising either of them.

BUILD A STRONG PORTFOLIO TO HIGHLIGHT YOUR SKILLS

Without an outstanding style, drone photos all look the same. You can naturally develop your style by taking lots of photos.

Experiment with different angles, heights, editing skills, and videography techniques. The more you do this, the closer you'll get to discovering your unique preferences.

Store all of your photos on a hard drive. As long as a picture is sharp and has a good composition, keep it.

You might come back to these outtakes and see potential in them.

If nothing else, you'll see where you went wrong and learn from it.

When you've already had a few photo shoots and feel confident in your work, you can start building your photography portfolio. Post your best work only.

Keep your photos diverse. This means you should take photos of different events and landscapes.

Show visitors all of your skills so that they can get inspired by your work. And if you inspire them, you're likely to be hired by them.

Draw up a Solid Pricing Plan to Avoid Confusion

There's no right or wrong way to create a photography pricing plan. Drone photographers can charge anywhere from $50 to $450 an hour. If you're a beginner and need experience, you'll probably want to start at a low rate.

Come up with a rate that seems fair to you. Now, compare it to your competitors' pricing packages. You have a right to charge more if you offer extra services.

Another thing to keep in mind is turnaround time.

If you can send your client the results within 24 hours, you should charge extra.

Some drone photographers offer a variety of pricing packages. Instead of charging per hour, you can offer an entire package for a fixed price.

Consider your turnaround time, how long you'll be photographing for, and if the clients want edited pictures or not.

Sell Your Photos on Stock Photo Websites for Extra Income

You don't always need to shoot for a client to earn some money. Many drone photographers sell their photos to publishers, advertising companies, and so on.

One of the easiest ways to do this is to find a stock photo agency.

You can submit exclusive or non-exclusive work. Exclusive work can be used only once or for a limited time.

Non-exclusive work can be bought over and over again.

Stock photo agencies don't usually pay as much as clients do, but they can be a great source of passive income.

Be Present on Social Media to Get More Exposure

Once everything is ready, you can start posting your photos on social media. Social media exposure can lead to more clients, a strong reputation, and paid promotions. It can also help you build a community of inspiring artists.

Start with a couple of social platforms. If you focus on just a few, you'll be able to spend your social media time wisely.

Post on a regular basis. Include people in your work so that they feel special. Use hashtags related to drone photography so more people can discover your work.

This might not always pay the bills, but it will keep you refreshed and motivated as a drone photographer.

Composition Tips For Drone Photography

Reasons to Try Bird's Eye View

Shooting from a bird's eye view gives your photos a whole new perspective. You can get some awe-inspiring images if you mindfully utilise this technique.

However, you need to make sure that you choose the right location and composition to bring the most out of your bird's eye view photos.

For this reason, we collected 8 ideas on how to use this point of view to boost your images.

To Give a Feeling of Power to Your Viewer

Photos that are taken from a bird's-eye view angle can make the viewer feel superior to the subject. When they look at the image, they feel powerful. They become the superhero who is looking down on the subject below.

You can use this effect to tell a story with your photos.

For example, if you photograph a child who has done something naughty, you can capture this from a bird's-eye view as if the viewer was the parent giving a lesson on good behaviour.

The bird's-eye perspective can make the viewer feel like they are protecting the subject who is below them. This can be a powerful tool when creating a photodocumentary.

By using this perspective, you can highlight how the viewer is more privileged than the subject of the photo.

It's also a good way to highlight the size of a crowd and make the viewer feel like they are standing above them. This can make them feel relieved, superior or even frustrated. It all depends on the impression you want to create.

To Highlight the Unique Pattern of a Landscape

When we are walking in a forest or a beach, we only see things from our own perspective. Many people never go above the trees or fly over the beach to get a bigger picture.

With bird's-eye view photography, you get a new perspective of the landscape. You can highlight textures and patterns that people wouldn't be able to see from eye level.

Think about the patterns of a pine tree forest from above. Or the waves and swirls creating uniques shapes in the ocean.

Landscapes can look completely different from a bird's-eye perspective.

To Capture Forms and Shapes From Above

Buildings often have interesting shapes and forms that we cannot see from the ground. But they showcase their pure beauty from above.

When you look at an architectural structure such as the Eiffel Tower or the Sagrada Familia from the ground, they look great. But you don't see the whole majestic structure.

If you go further away and climb to a higher lookout point, these buildings pop out from the rest of the cityscape. They become breathtaking masterpieces of architecture.

To Discover the Symmetry of a Cityscape

Cities and urban areas are often built in perfect symmetry. But this is something we cannot recognize when we are walking in the street.

Go above the city and capture its symmetry from a bird's perspective.

You can use drones or take pictures. But you can also go to a higher spot in the city, and capture the cityscape from that point.

To Capture the Full Scale of Impressive Landscapes

There are landscapes that look stunning from where we stand. But they look even more majestic from a bird's-eye view. The best examples are the mountainous landscapes.

When you shoot the mountains from a bird's-eye view, you often capture peaks in the foreground and in the background as well. This creates depth of field and highlights the altitude differences.

Add a human element for scale, and you create the most stunning mountain photography from above.

To Provide an Exciting Perspective of Mainstream Scenes

There are scenes we see every single day, and we don't even care about giving them a second glance. Road junctions, basketball fields or parks have the same old boring look.

But shoot these scenes from a different perspective, and a whole new world opens up.

Try to capture them from a 40-degree or a 90-degree bird's-eye view. They will showcase patterns, lines and forms that you wouldn't normally see.

A serpentine road doesn't look spectacular from the ground.

But go a bit higher and take photos of it from above. Its curvy shape will look stunning from that higher angle.

To Turn Dull Cityscapes into Pieces of Art

After a while, every cityscape seems to look the same. Skyscrapers, big buildings, busy streets.

It's hard to distinguish one from another. Plus, famous cities like New York City or London have been photographed thousands of times.

But you can give an exciting twist to the well-known cityscapes by changing the perspective.

Go for the bird's-eye view photography and capture these cities from an overhead perspective.

To Transport Your Viewer to Beautiful Scenes

One of the biggest advantages of bird's-eye photography is the way you can make the viewer feel.

The freedom you give them by capturing these scenes from above is priceless.

They would have to hop on an aeroplane to see forests, roads and cities from above.

Instead, your photos provide them with the opportunity to see scenes like never before.

You can make the viewer feel free as a bird, flying over landscapes and cityscapes towards the horizon.

The best photographs are those that make people think or trigger emotions in them.

PROCESSING YOUR DRONE PHOTOGRAPHY

How to Edit Photos in Photoshop

Getting started with editing is a tricky area of photography. There are so many filters, tools and adjustments you can use that it becomes hard to navigate between your options.

Even if you are new to photography, you have heard of Photoshop. This programme is the perfect tool for altering, correcting and manipulating your images.

In drone photography, you will also feel the need to start editing your images.

Photoshop is one of the most versatile editing softwares out there. But it's also one of the most intimidating because of its huge amount of photo editing tools.

Make Non-Destructive Edits With Photoshop Layers

One of the most powerful editing tools in Photoshop (PS) are layers. Layers are like sheets of paper that are stacked one on top of the other. There is a panel dedicated to layers.

When you open a photo in PS, you will just have the Background layer. This corresponds to the original photo.

Each layer you add will contain an adjustment or a part of the picture you are creating.

For example, on top of the background layer, you can add a layer that increases the exposure (read Tip 2 if you want to learn how it's done).

On top of those two, you can add even more layers to make other adjustments to the photo like vibrance, saturation, etc.

You can stack as many layers as you like. The final photo is the result of all the layers together.

In Photoshop, if you work directly on your background picture, any change you do modifies the pixels of the original photo.

You should know that depending on the changes you make in the picture, you might not be able to undo it.

Setting up and editing through layers will allow you to edit your photo in a non-destructive way. This means that you can come back to the original one at any time. This is the best way to edit photos.

My first recommendation is to extra protect your original by always creating a first layer that simply duplicates it by pressing Ctrl+J (Cmd+J for mac users).

Then you can start adding other layers on top with your modifications.

Layers add a lot of flexibility to the workflow because you can:

- reorganise them (by click and dragging them);

- rename them by clicking on the layer's name;

- modulate their intensity by adjusting their Opacity (using the Opacity slide);

- activate and deactivate them to check their effect (clicking on the eye icon);

- and delete them (dragging them to the trash icon).

Edit Pictures Using Adjustment Layers

An adjustment layer is an editing tool that allows you to do different types of modifications to your images. You can add them in two ways.

Click on the icon in the layer panel and then choose one of the adjustment layer options.

Or go to Layer>New adjustment layer and select one of the options.

The adjustment layer will appear on top of the previous ones you have. You can modify the adjustment using its properties panel. The changes will affect all the layers below.

There are so many adjustment layer types that you might feel a bit overwhelmed.

Focus on some of the fundamental adjustments until you get used to

Photoshop and feel like experimenting with others.

Some suitable options that affect the tonal range or the colour of your photo are Exposure, Curves, Vibrance or Hue/Saturation.

Select Areas of Your Images With the Marquee and Lasso Tools

You can select areas of your images in several different ways. For selecting areas with specific shapes, you can use the Marquee tool. There is a rectangular shaped one.

After right-clicking on the icon, you can select the Elliptical shape or even a single row/column Marquee tool.

You select the area by clicking on the starting point and dragging the cursor across the photo until you reach the desired size.

Another way of selecting areas is by using the Lasso Tool. With this feature, you can select a free area in your images. There are several types of Lasso Tools.

With the Basic one (Lasso Tool) you can select areas by freehand. The Polygonal Lasso allows you to create edges by clicking on points.

The Magnetic option is great to select along edges. Click on the starting point of the selection and move your mouse.

You will see that the selection line wrap the edge and Photoshop add points along the course of the mouse. You can add points by clicking with the mouse or delete them by clicking the delete button.

With any of the lasso tools, to complete the selection, you need to get to the first point and close the "circle".

A great feature for selecting big uniform areas is the Magic Wand Tool. It is under the Quick Selection Tool, so you need to right-click and select it from the menu.

The mouse will turn into a magic wand.

If you click on a spot, it will select all the similar ones. Doing so, it can select big areas at once.

You might have some spots that remain not selected. If so, press Shift while you click on them with the magic wand and they will also be added to the selection. And if you want to remove any selection, you just need to press Ctrl+D (or Cmd+D in a Mac).

Use Masks to Edit Just a Portion of Your Photo

Masks allow you to make adjustments in just a selection of your photo.

A mask "protects" the selected pixels from any editing tools you use in the adjustment layer.

Masks are automatically added with the adjustment curves. The mask is the white square next to the adjustment layer icon. When working with masks. you play with the colours white and black.

White means that the pixel is active, so it is affected by the adjustment layer modifications. Black means that you mask it, meaning that the pixel is not affected by the adjustment layer. But how to use white and black? With the brush tool, you add the mask by painting in black.

Pick a brush icon and adjust its size and hardness in the menu. Make sure you have the black colour selected.

You will see that you are not adding black to the photo. You are adding black onto the mask to indicate the pixels you don't want to be affected by the adjustment layer (transparent).

If you paint too much or you want to correct something, you can do it by painting in white.

There is also another way to create a mask. First, select the area you want to mask and while the selection is active, create the adjustment layer. Photoshop will automatically create the mask with the selection.

Learn to Straighten a Crooked Photo

Straightening a crooked photo in Photoshop is easy. First, you need to use the Measure tool. If you don´t see it in your palette, it might be hidden under the Eyedropper tool.

To select it you need to right-click on the Eyedropper icon. A little menu appears with the other photo editing tools hidden behind.

We need to find in our photo a line that was supposed to be straight. It might

be the horizon, a wall, a table. It will depend on the content of your image.

Now we need to draw a line along with it.

Click on one side of the line and drag over the line until you reach to the end and then click again. Photoshop measures the angle of this line in reference to the rest of the image. You can see the result in the Options Bar Menu.

Now select Image>Rotate Canvas>Arbitrary and write the angle you obtained. Photoshop automatically fills with the obtained measurements the options in the Rotate Canvas Menu.

Just check that they are correct and press OK.

When you straighten an image, it is common that you get some white canvas around. You can get rid of it by cropping the image with the Crop Tool. Click on one corner of the image and drag until you get the area you want to keep.

Then press Enter/Return to crop.

Lighten and Darken Just Certain Parts of Your Image.

You can use the Dodge tool for making portions of the images lighter. This is handy when you don't like the exposure you got straight from the camera.

When you select the icon, you can choose in the toolbar if aiming to the shadows, mid-tones or highlights.

Photoshop will selectively lighten just those ones. You need to go over the area you want to make brighter with a brush.

Remove Unwanted Objects With Content-Aware

There are different ways to Photoshop images to remove unwanted objects. One of my favourites is using the Content-Aware option.

Start by selecting the area with unwanted objects with any selecting tool. Just make sure you are not in an adjustment layer when you make the selection.

I like using the Lasso option. Once selected, right-click and choose 'Fill'.

A panel appears, and I select "Content-Aware" and "Normal" in Blending. I keep the Opacity at 100. Photoshop is going to fill the area with the content it decides on after searching surrounding areas.

And most of the times it does a pretty good job.

Add a Vignette to Drive Attention to the Centre of the Images

Vignette means darkening the corners of a photo. It drives the viewer's attention to the centre of the image.

You don't have to add a vignette to all your images, but in some cases, it provides a nice result.

Try not to exaggerate with it to keep a natural look.

Select the central area of your image. You are selecting the part that won't have the vignette. Use the Elliptical marquee to do it.

Feather the selection to create a gradual darkening effect. Go to Select>Modify>Feather.

In the Feather Selection menu, you need to write a feather radius. It will depend on the image size, and you might need some trial and error.

In my case, a radius of 200 pixels worked fine. Photoshop will blur those pixels, making them blend with the background in a more natural way.

Now you need to invert the selection going to Select>Inverse.

Then add a curves adjustment layer and play around until you get the vignetting effect you like.

Save Photos in PSD to Keep All Your Changes

A very important part of photo editing is saving your file. If you want to keep editing later, you can save it as a Photoshop file (psd). This file will keep all your edits and layers.

Keep in mind that it has a huge file size. Go to File>Save and select PSD from all the options.

Use this option if you want to keep all the quality of the Photoshop file. If you want a smaller file, you can save your image as TIFF.

That is another of the options in the "Save as" menu.

You will lose all the edit's history and layers, so don't save it in TIFF until you are sure you finished all the photo editing!

Although the TIFF file is smaller than the Photoshop, it is still pretty big for using in websites or sharing in social media. In that case, you will need a compressed file as the JPG.

When you select it in the "Save as" menu and click "Save", a window will appear:

You can select the quality. The higher the quality, the bigger the file.

Now you need to decide what it is more important to you on each occasion.

If you want the photos for the web, you have another option for saving them.

Go to File>Save for Web. In this panel, you will be able to select the image quality and its size.

The most interesting thing is that you can put your original and the final jpg side by side (in the 2-Up tab) to see how the changes will affect it.

Use Photoshop Shortcuts to Save Time

My last tip is not about photo editing itself. But it saved me a lot of time sitting in front of the computer.

It also simplified my photo editing flow. I highly recommend you to invest some time learning Photoshop keyboard shortcuts for the tools you use the most.

It requires some memory effort at first, but believe me: it is totally worth it.

You can make a list with the shortcuts you use the most. You can have it close to you when you edit a photo to check the list when you need it.

Best Photo Stitching Software

Creating panoramic images might be one reason why you bought your drone in the first place.

Many editing programmes will help you create spectacular panorama images. Many of them are intuitive to use when stitching images together.

Hugin

Hugin is a photo stitching software capable of assembling a mosaic of photographs into a panorama.

Hugin's interface is functional and user friendly. The software has great features. Some of them are control points or corrections of inconsistent levels. Manual adjustments of projections are also included.

Hugin offers a series of online tutorials in 9 languages. They show the different stages of the panorama

stitching process. And they teach you how to use blend masks and create textures.

Hugin is an open-source initiative. It is available for free and is compatible with Windows, Mac, or Linux.

PTGui

PTGui is the best choice for professional-level photo stitching software. PTGui allows for stitching panoramas with many rows and columns.

PTGui has a less expensive option that will offer plenty for amateur photographers. The more expensive version, PTGui Pro, gives added features that any pro would love.

PTGui Pro includes features like Automatic Seam Placement and a Fill-Holes function. PTGui Pro also offers a Batch Stitcher, which can generate control points to set up a panorama.

You can also stitch and blend HDR source images into an HDR panorama with PTGui Pro.

Viewpoint correction and masking are also included.

PTGui works with Windows, Mac, or Linux.

There is a free trial version and a one-time license fee.

Panoweaver 10

Panoweaver 10 offers a standard and pro version. The standard version offers a good amount of features.

They include gigapixel panoramas, little planet panoramas, and full manual adjustments.

For a bit more of an investment, the Pro version has added features. These include HDR processing, masking, and Dehaze.

One of the biggest benefits of Panoweaver 10 is that it offers the option of automatic stitching.

This is great for those of us who sometimes want to be less hands-on.

AutoStitch

Autostitch lets you stitch many photos into a seamless panoramic image.

This photo stitching software is the perfect solution if you want a program that will do it all for you.

It requires no user input to sift through images. AutoStitch selects the images that match up. Then it pieces them together to create a panorama.

The downside to this is that if you do want to make individual adjustments, you cannot.

AutoStitch is ideal for the photographer who doesn't do too many panoramas.

And it's also good if you are not looking to control every aspect of its creation.

A demo version of this photo stitching software is available for free. As a standalone, AutoStitch is available for Windows and Mac OS X.

PanoramaStudio

PanoramaStudio is photo stitching software available for Windows and Mac. There is a standard and pro version.

The latter offers a few more options, like support for ultra-wide-angle and fish-eye lenses.

This software offers interactive tools that allow you to add hotspots to panoramic images and create virtual tours.

PanoramaStudio allows you to export interactive panoramas to HTML5. It also offers multiple editing tools to correct flaws and enhance your pictures.

This software is perfect if you usually work with Adobe Lightroom. You can find it as a Lightroom plugin.

Panorama Stitcher

This photo stitching software is a fantastic option for Mac users. A mini-version is available for free, but it can only stitch together up to five photos.

For panoramas of more than five photos, you will need to buy the full version of Panorama Stitcher.

It doesn't compare to the detailed control you have in other software options like PTGui.

But in true Mac fashion, it is very user-friendly.

It is currently available for Macs only via the App Store.

PhotoStitcher

Another fantastic option for beginners in photo stitching is PhotoStitcher. It features a user-friendly interface and an entire suite of software to alter images.

PhotoStitcher is capable of stitching photos of different angles or resolutions. It also does automatic image completion.

This panorama stitching software also automates things like cropping and exposure balancing.

This gives you the option to be as hands-off as you'd like.

A free trial download is available. The full PhotoStitcher software is affordably priced.

GigaPan Stitch

If you're dedicated to taking photos of landscapes and panoramas, you may already own GigaPan Epic hardware. If that is the case, then you're aware of GigaPan Stitch software.

GigaPan Stitch is a functional panorama stitching software. It combines photos across many rows and columns.

It is proprietary and only for use with GigaPan hardware. But it provides a great option to stay within the GigaPan product family.

This software is basic. Yet, it is capable of stitching together panoramas with many rows of images.

Once you register your GigaPan hardware, you receive a license key for the stitching software. If you want to test it out before committing, a free 14-day trial available for download.

CONCLUSION

Drone filmmaking and photography have become increasingly popular in recent years and have transformed the video production industry. They provide a unique perspective on many areas.

Aside from allowing enthusiasts to take pictures and movies from incredible viewpoints, drones provide even more variety by allowing users to add distinctive visual components to help convey a message.

While not a standalone panorama photo stitcher software, Photoshop is a good choice. It has powerful photo stitching capabilities within its arsenal of features.

Photoshop's Photomerge plugin is basic but handy for the occasional panorama.

You can access the photo stitching option in the menus (File > Automate > Photomerge). This will open a new window where can you add the individual photos to be merged.

Also, choose the geometric projection, and select a few minor options.

The plugin will then do the stitching for you!

Once merged, the new file is a PSD file with separate layers for each image.

One downside to using the Photoshop Photomerge plugin is that it's not very detailed in its controls.

Since you are already working within Photoshop, you will have all the tools to finesse the image. You don't need separate software.

Photoshop is not an ideal photo stitching solution if you offer many panoramas commercially. Yet, it is perfect for those of us who do the occasional panorama for fun.

Photoshop is available for Windows or Mac. You can access this cloud-based software with a monthly or yearly plan.